NATURE ADVENTURES

# GOING FISHING

Madison Parker

NorwoodHouse Press

**Cataloging-in-Publication Data**

Names: Parker, Madison.
Title: Going fishing / Madison Parker.
Description: Buffalo, NY : Norwood House Press, 2026. | Series: Nature adventures | Includes glossary and index.
Identifiers: ISBN 9781978574656 (pbk.) | ISBN 9781978574663 (library bound) | ISBN 9781978574670 (ebook)
Subjects: LCSH: Fishing--Juvenile literature.
Classification: LCC SH445.P375 2026 | DDC 799.1--dc23

Published in 2026 by
**Norwood House Press**
2544 Clinton Street
Buffalo, NY 14224


Designer: Rhea Magaro
Editor: Kim Thompson

Photo credits: Cover, p. 1 titov dmitriy/Shutterstock.com; p. 5 Shakirov Albert/Shutterstock.com; pp. 6, 21 SeventyFour/Shutterstock.com; p. 7 MintImages/Shutterstock.com; pp. 8,9 gresei/Shutterstock.com; p. 10 Mariya Surmacheva/Shutterstock.com; p. 11 martellostudio/Shutterstock.com; p. 12 Photobyt/Shutterstock.com;p. 13 Matt Jeppson/Shutterstock.com; p. 15 BearFotos/Shutterstock.com; p. 16 samray/Shutterstock.com; p. 17 art4you1/Shutterstock.com; p. 18 lunamarina/Shutterstock.com; p. 19 dba87/Shutterstock.com;



Printed in the United States of America



CPSIA compliance information: Batch #CSNHP26: For further information contact Norwood House Press at 1-800-237-9932.

# TABLE OF CONTENTS

## WHAT IS FISHING?

Let's go fishing! Fishing is a fun outdoor activity.

Fishing is when people try to catch wild fish. Many people enjoy fishing adventures.

Some fishers stand on the shore. Some go out in boats. They try to catch all kinds of fish. They hope they will have good luck!

# FISHING SUPPLIES

You will need a fishing rod and **reel**. Fishing line is stored in the reel. The rod is used to **cast** the line into the water.

**Bait** goes on a hook at the end of the line. It can be a live animal like a worm. It can be a **lure**. A fish bites the bait and gets caught on the hook. Then, the fisher reels the fish in.

Sinkers are weights you can attach to the fishing line. They make the bait sink down to where the fish are.

A bobber floats. When a fish bites, the bobber gets pulled underwater.

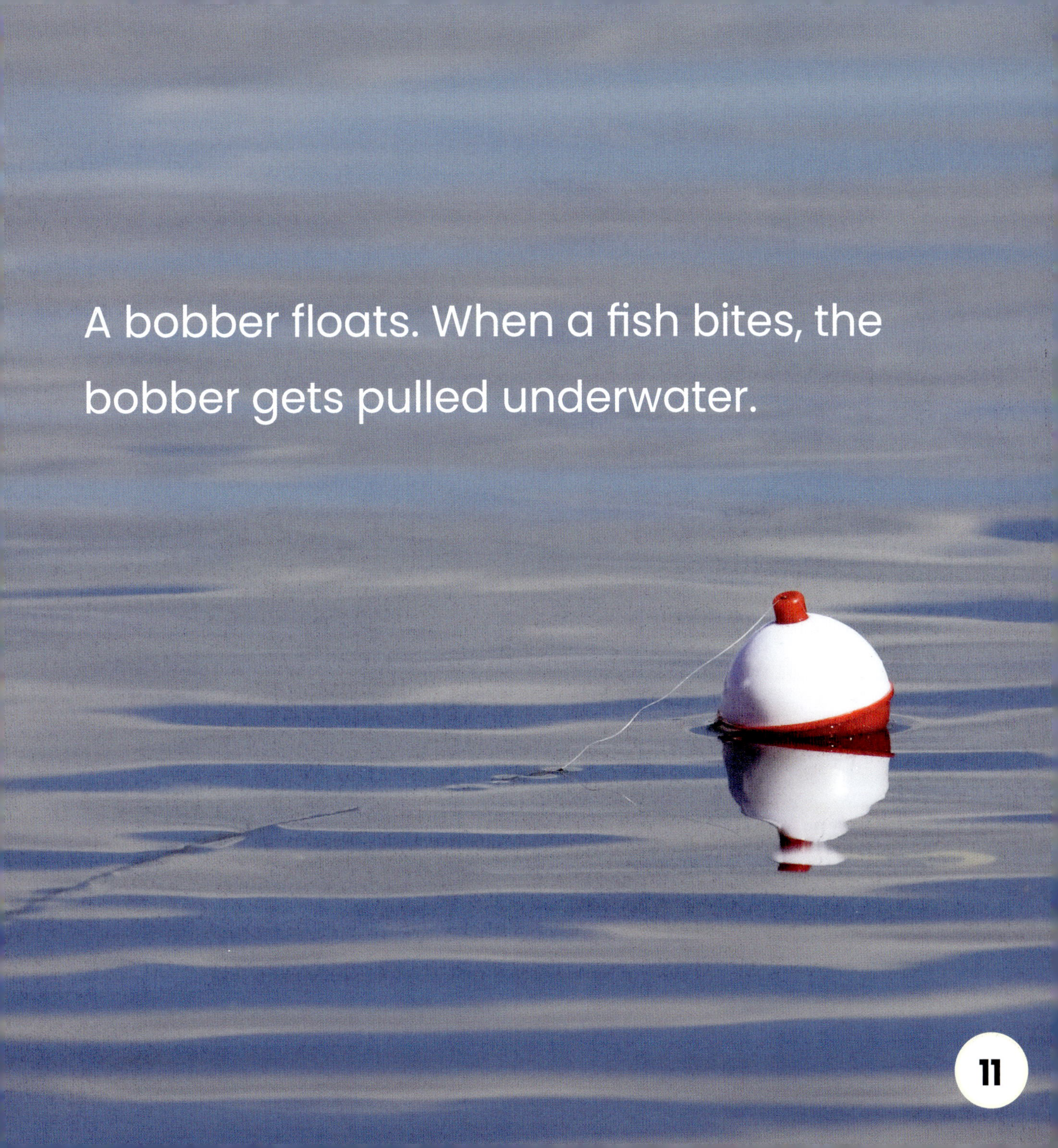

In many places, you need a fishing **license**. You can get one through a government office or a store that sells fishing gear.

Fishers should wear a hat for protection from the sun. Some fishers wear **waders** when they walk out into the water.

## FISHING SAFETY

It is important to be safe when you go fishing. Hooks are sharp. Be careful when you bait hooks or remove them from fish. Fishing line is strong. Make sure to handle it carefully.

Fishers should Leave No **Trace** (LNT). That means you should not leave trash or anything else behind.

Leave the **wilderness** better than you found it. This protects **wildlife**.

## WHERE TO GO FISHING

There are many good places to fish.

You can fish in a stream, lake, or river.

You can fish in the ocean.

It is important to read any **regulations** before you go.

You can visit your state's park website to find fishing spots near you. Fishing helps you explore the great outdoors!

# Glossary

**bait** (bayt): food or a lure that is put on a hook and used to catch fish

**cast** (kast): to throw

**license** (LYE-suhns): a document that gives you official permission to do something

**lure** (loor): artificial bait that is used to catch fish and that often looks like a worm or an insect

**reel** (reel): a spool on which fishing line is wound; to wind up fishing line in order to pull in a fish after it has been hooked

**regulations** (reg-yuh-LAY-shuhnz): rules you need to follow

**trace** (trays): a sign that someone has been in a place; evidence

**waders** (WAY-durz): waterproof pants and boots fishers wear to walk into the water without getting wet

**wilderness** (WIL-dur-nis): wild land where no people live

**wildlife** (WILDE-life): wild animals living in their natural environment

# Thinking Questions

1. What is fishing?
2. What do people use to catch fish?
3. What is the purpose of sinkers?
4. Why is it important to be careful around fishing hooks?
5. Where can you go fishing?

# Index



# About the Author

**Madison Parker** spent her childhood in the city of Chicago, Illinois. A farm girl at heart, today she lives in Wisconsin with her husband and four children on a small farm with cows, goats, chickens, and two miniature horses named Harley and David. Her favorite dessert is vanilla frozen custard with rainbow sprinkles, even in the winter.